FAITH AND
TRANSFORMATION
FRIDAYS
A FAITH WORKBOOK

I0458614

LEAH AYANNA JOHNSON, PH.D.

www.TrueVinePublishing.org

Faith and Transformation Fridays
Leah Ayanna Johnson, Ph.D.

Published by
True Vine Publishing Co.
810 Dominican Dr.
Nashville, TN 37228
www.TrueVinePublishing.org

Copyright © 2025 by Leah Ayanna Johnson, Ph.D.
All rights reserved. No part of this book may be reproduced in any form or by any electronic or mechanical means, including information storage and retrieval or mechanical means without permission in writing from the publisher, except by a reviewer who may quote brief passages in a review.

ISBN: 978-1-962783-62-0 Paperback
ISBN: 978-1-962783-63-7 eBook

Scripture quotations marked KJV are taken from the Holy Bible King James Version

Scripture quotations marked "ESV" are from the ESV® Bible (The Holy Bible, English Standard Version®), copyright © 2001 by Crossway, a publishing ministry of Good News Publishers. Used by permission. All rights reserved. You may not copy or download more than 500 consecutive verses of the ESV Bible or more than one half of any book of the ESV Bible.

Scripture taken from the New King James Version®. Copyright © 1982 by Thomas Nelson. Used by permission. All rights reserved.

*F*aith and Transformation Fridays is a faith workbook that provides readers with biblical and experiential faith references woven into an encouraging and inspiring narrative. This book guides readers through a year of applicable faith practices rooted in testimony and scripture. It shares true-life experiences, the Word of God, and the Word of faith, demonstrating that faith in Christ Jesus leads to transformation.

Designed with blank journal entry spaces after each chapter, *Faith and Transformation Fridays* allows for personal reflection and application. It encourages faith in practice and serves as a personal journal for manifesting faith in the reader's life.

This book began as a weekly podcast series until it became evident, by the unction of the Holy Ghost, that it needed to be a book—a processing journal for others to walk their journey of faith in practice. I pray for God's revelation in your life as you embark on this reflective journey.

TABLE OF CONTENTS

INTRODUCTION

The phone rang in the middle of the day while I was at work. It was a call from someone I had not expected. I answered, unsure of what to expect from the voice on the other end.

They stated, "I am on assignment, and I will be brief. Are you still believing God for your heart's desire?"

I replied, "Yes, I still believe."

They responded, "Okay. How you answered that question determined how I would respond. God will grant you according to your faith."

"God will grant you according to your faith." Those words continue to resonate with me to this day as I apply them to every area of my life.

CHAPTER ONE

STANDING ON THE WORD OF GOD

Welcome to *Faith and Transformation Fridays.* Hopefully, you have made it through your week well, it is Friday, and you are ready to rest, reflect, and travel with me.

As many of you may or may not know, I am an entrepreneur, public speaker, and author. I have authored three books, started a nonprofit, and launched a for-profit organization. Over the past 20 years, I have developed businesses and organizations while pursuing various creative ventures. Recently, I found myself on a life-altering faith journey. I'm talking about faith in Christ Jesus—the kind of faith that has transformed every area of my life. This journey, while rewarding, has at times felt like a roller coaster ride with its ups and downs, but it has also brought me experiences I am eager to share with you. Come with me as I take you down the road of my journey, and together we embark on this faith adventure.

At the time of this entry, and for the five years preceding it, I had been intently listening to and learning from God. Life has taken many turns. I have experienced profound changes, and now it's time to share those experiences with you in the hope that you, too, will be encouraged. Before beginning any journey, you need a foundation to ground you along the way. So, I ask: *What are you standing on?*

Our scripture reference for this chapter is Deuteronomy 28:13:

"And the Lord shall make thee the head, and not the tail; and thou shalt be above only, and thou shalt not be beneath; if that thou hearken unto the commandments of the Lord thy God, which I command thee this day, to observe and to do them." (King James Bible, 1769/2017, Deuteronomy 28:13)

I have always known I was called to lead, but I first had to learn to follow. For many years, I worked to help build companies and organizations. I enjoyed my work in the education and nonprofit sectors; I truly loved what I did. As I advanced in my career, receiving promotions and competitive salaries, I became comfortable. However, I sensed that it was time to move on. I felt the pull to step into a role as CEO or Executive Director elsewhere, knowing that such experience would prepare me to lead my own organization someday.

Before I knew it, I was standing at a crossroads. Although I was in a comfortable job, I felt the tugging of the Holy Spirit, urging me to leave. Yes, you read that right—I left my well-paying, comfortable job because I knew it was time to move forward. This decision was not easy, but I clung to God's promise in Deuteronomy 28:13: *"He will make you the head and not the tail."* I knew that this promise applied to me. I understood that God had gifted me in administration and called me to lead. Yet, stepping out of my comfort zone to follow His lead was one of the scariest things I've ever done.

I had to put my faith in God's Word. If He said He would make me the head and not the tail, then I had to trust Him to fulfill that promise. I prayed and reminded myself of His Word: *"God, you told me to be the head and not the tail."* For years, I had dedicated myself to developing someone else's organization, but now it was time to take a risk and pursue what God had called me to do.

This journey may not be the same steps God has for you—and that's okay. These were the steps I knew He was leading me to take. It was time for growth and stretching. I had to leave the comfort of what was familiar to follow God's leading. Faith compels us to follow. You can't be an effective leader without first learning how to follow and support others. Faith teaches us how to follow God and trust Him for our next steps.

Faith in Christ Jesus means saying, "Okay, God, I trust You. I believe You. I've been diligent where I am, and now it's time to move forward." Faith will cause you to stand on His Word without seeing the outcome. I had to stand on the promise that He would make me the head and not the tail, that He would provide for me, and that there is a season for everything. Even though I didn't have another position lined up, I chose to leave my comfortable job to pursue my dream and vision.

> "FAITH IS A JOURNEY—A JOURNEY TO TRUST, BELIEVE, AND GROW—IF YOU ARE WILLING TO TAKE IT."

The decision to leave what was familiar was one of faith and obedience. I submitted my resignation to pursue a path that had not yet materialized, trusting that God had greater things in store for me. The job shift was just one part of my testimony. Throughout this workbook, I will share other segments of my story—the roller coaster ride of faith that brought transformation. I hope to motivate and encourage you to trust God. When you stand on faith, transformation comes. Faith is a journey—a journey to trust, believe, and grow—if you are willing to take it. This chapter, *Standing on the Word,* is based on Deuteronomy 28:13 (King James Bible, 1769/2017). As always, we will close with prayer.

Prayer:

Father God, in the name of Jesus, I ask that whoever reads this would be encouraged and motivated to trust in You and Your promises. May they find rest in Your Word and take the risks necessary to walk through this faith journey. I pray that they grow and develop into the magnificent people You have designed them to be. Lord, thank You for the opportunity to come together and for the transformation that faith brings.
In Your holy name, Jesus Christ, I pray. Amen.

Until next Friday…

JOURNAL ENTRY

This is your opportunity to reflect, apply the scripture references to your life, list concrete ways to apply this chapter's scripture references, or ask God questions pertaining to your life and faith walk. As you write, expect God to respond. Be ready to be still and to listen.

_____

_____

_____

_____

_____

_____

_____

_____

_____

_____

_____

_____

_____

_____

_____

_____

_____

_____

_____

_____

_____

CHAPTER TWO

BOLD ENOUGH TO BELIEVE

This Friday, let's examine if we are bold enough to believe. Our scripture references are found in Luke 17:5-6 and Matthew 17:19-20(King James Bible, 1769/2017).

"And the apostles said unto the Lord, Increase our faith. And the Lord said, If ye had faith as a grain of mustard seed, ye might say unto this sycamine tree, Be thou plucked up by the root, and be thou planted in the sea; and it should obey you." (King James Bible, 1769/2017, Luke 17:5-6)

"Then came the disciples to Jesus apart, and said, Why could not we cast him out? And Jesus said unto them, Because of your unbelief: for verily I say unto you, If ye have faith as a grain of mustard seed, ye shall say unto this mountain, Remove hence to yonder place; and it shall remove, and nothing shall be impossible unto you." (*King James Bible,* 1769/2017, Matthew 17:19-20)

"WE CAN SUMMON SOMETHING THAT HAS NEVER EXISTED, AND IT MUST OBEY US."

I love these scripture references because they show me the power of faith when you believe, have faith in God, and operate fully in the measure of faith that God has given to every human being. Anything we say is possible to us. We can command the impossible to move, and it will be done. We can summon something that has never existed, and it must obey us. However, if we operate in unbelief, there are things we cannot achieve. We must ask God to increase our faith so that we can fully operate in the area where we are called to function.

In the previous chapter, I shared how I left a plush job that paid me well, but I walked away because of the calling to do something greater. It was a calling to stretch myself professionally, create a career, and secure an executive position before it was even established. When others thought I was crazy, I had to stand on the word of God. After resigning from my good and comfortable position, I had to be bold enough to trust God to fulfill what I believed Him to do.

I had to be bold enough to pitch an idea for a company—an organization—in an environment where the people did not look like me or share my background. Our parents did not attend the same schools or country clubs. I worked in an environment vastly different from my own, yet I had to persuade those board executives to support an idea they were familiar with but had little interest in implementing in that geographical location.

I had to do the legwork. I was creating an executive position for myself to grow personally and professionally while launching a franchise for the first time for this organization. I knew I was called to leadership and needed to grow in that capacity. I recognized my gift in administration, and I desired more. I took a risk. I did not know if the board members would say, *"We're not going to support this"* or, *"We're not backing it financially."* I also didn't know if they would dismiss it altogether due to their lack of interest in that geographical location. But I had already resigned from my comfortable leadership position to pursue this. I took the risk.

There were so many variables that could have changed at any time during the process, but I was bold enough to believe God. *Ask, and it shall be given.* I was bold enough to trust that this was the time and season to move forward. I said, *"Lord, I believe You will answer my prayer for a greater position."* I believed in God enough to step into this newly proposed position, so much so that I relinquished my comfortable position.

During that time, I was feeding my faith and commanding my actions to align with that faith. I worked diligently to persuade the board members. I had to do the legwork to create the executive position and prove that what I envisioned was possible. People who initially doubted me saw my seriousness, and eventually, they chose to back me.

What are you willing to give up to see your faith manifest what you believe?

By the grace of God and through my faith in Him, I was able to create an executive position for myself. There are opportunities available to you—ones that may not be visible right now, may not yet be created, or may not even exist in the job description you're pursuing. You may need to do some legwork, research, or pitch ideas. You may have to persuade others and pour your energy into your vision.

> **"WHAT ARE YOU WILLING TO GIVE UP TO SEE YOUR FAITH MANIFEST WHAT YOU BELIEVE?"**

If you are bold enough to believe God's word—if He said it, then it will be so (Numbers 23:19, King James Version, 1769/2017). If you have faith that nothing is impossible for you, then it shall not be impossible (Luke 1:37, King James Version, 1769/2017).

That is part of my testimony. I know it sounds crazy—I left something great and created a wonderful position for myself—but my testimony does not end there. Trust me, there is more to this roller-coaster ride. There is a blessing in the faith journey!

I encourage you: if you hear from God, trust Him. If your desires align with His will and His word, then nothing will be withheld from you. Be bold enough to believe God's word.

Prayer:

Father God, in the name of Jesus Christ, we thank You for the opportunity to stand on faith, to operate in faith, and to see transformation in our lives. Thank You for planting this word on good ground in our spirits so we can be bold enough to believe Your promises, bold enough to believe Your word, and bold enough to see Your word fulfilled in our lives.

God, I pray for every reader, that they may grow in the knowledge of Your truth and be continually blessed as they walk in faith. As it says in the scriptures, let it be in us: increase our faith so that whatever we declare, it must obey. God, we thank You and praise Your holy name today. In Jesus' name, we pray. Amen.

Until next Friday…

JOURNAL ENTRY

This is your opportunity to reflect, apply the scripture references to your life, list concrete ways to apply this chapter's scripture references, or ask God questions pertaining to your life and faith walk. As you write, expect God to respond. Be ready to be still and to listen.

_____

_____

_____

_____

_____

_____

_____

_____

_____

_____

_____

_____

_____

_____

_____

_____

_____

_____

_____

_____

_____

_____

CHAPTER THREE

WALK IN IT

"God is not a man, that he should lie; neither the son of man, that he should repent: hath he said, and shall he not do it? or hath he spoken, and shall he not make it good?" (Numbers 23:19, King James Bible, 1769/2017))

Standing on the Word of God took on another dimension of meaning. Now, I had to walk in the faith of the Lord. In this phase of my career, I was walking in an executive position that I had been able to create for myself. I was operating fully in the role, learning from the experiences, and growing. In the midst of where I was, I had to trust that where I was, was where I belonged. I belonged there, and that position belonged to me. If others could do it for their own endeavors, then I could do it as well.

I came to a point where I learned that I had to own what faith said I could have, even in the midst of doubting faces, unbelieving comments, snide remarks, and incredulous expressions. Many people around me who had worked with me for years were comfortable with me when I was their support, their second-in-command, or when I was advising them on how to grow their companies. Now that I had branched out on my own and was the lead authority, my actions and assumption of the role were being questioned. Some colleagues wondered if my new role or title was simply a matter of "semantics." Others, who had previously trusted me, suddenly had doubts, asking,

"Are you able to do this job?"

It's worth noting that these doubts didn't arise because of any failure or wrongdoing on my part. It was simply that I had been elevated to operate in a new capacity.

You have to be able to stand on your faith in the midst of doubting faces and comments. I had to own my leadership in the face of racism, sexism, and doubtful inquiries. I was bombarded with this power struggle on a professional level. I experienced every "-ism" you can imagine in a way I had never encountered before. I had to fight against the externally imposed impostor syndrome—the thoughts of "I don't know if I can."

I realized I could not internalize the doubts of others simply because of their jealousy, unbelief, or own struggle for power. I could not entertain their doubtful questions or make them my own. Remember the scripture in Numbers 23:19 (King James Bible, 1769/2017). I know that if God called me to a position in administration and leadership, then He called me there to grow, develop, and do it well.

I had to own my faith. I had to walk in the truth that yes, I was an executive. Yes, I had the necessary skills, experience, and talents to do the job, and yes, it was my time. I was able to get people to invest in an area they had previously ignored. I launched an organization in a place where others had only talked about the idea but never acted on it.

It is important to record your successes because you need to remind yourself:

- I am successful through Christ Jesus.
- I can do all things through Christ Jesus, who strengthens me.
- My faith in Him says that with Him, all things are possible.
- Behold, I am made new.

When you begin to walk in the faith that God has placed in your life and fully accept His Word, you must learn to record your successes. These successes will help quench every doubtful thought, jealous or negative statement, and every form of "-ism" (racism, sexism) you may encounter.

I encourage you by sharing a small portion of my testimony about my faith journey in my career. This is just one aspect of my life that I'm sharing. Whatever area of your life God has placed you in—where you are passionate and aligned with His will and purpose for your life—walk in it!

> "WHEN YOU WALK IN *HIS* FAITH, A TRANSFORMATION OCCURS IN YOUR THOUGHTS, HEART, ACTIONS, AND SPEECH..

Whether it's your marriage, your relationships, your parenting, your career, your visions, your dreams, or your plans, you have the ability to walk in the faith of Christ Jesus. You can do it. Know that when you walk in *His* faith, a transformation occurs in your thoughts, heart, actions, and speech. Everything will follow!

This Friday, I encourage you to walk in it. Walk in the faith of Christ Jesus. Walk in the promises of God. Walk in your purpose with pride, confidence, and security, standing on the Word found in Numbers 23:19 (King James Bible, 1769/2017).

Prayer:

Father God, in the name of Jesus Christ, thank you, thank you, thank you. Thank you for this reminder that we can walk in faith, believing in You, Christ Jesus. We can walk in Your promises. We can walk in the faith of Your purpose for our lives, and we can do it with confidence and security. We thank You right now for allowing this Word to take root on good ground in our spirit so it may bring forth good fruit in our lives. Lord, we thank You and praise Your holy name right now. In Jesus' name, we pray, Amen.

Until next Friday...

JOURNAL ENTRY

This is your opportunity to reflect, apply the scripture references to your life, list concrete ways to apply this chapter's scripture references, or ask God questions pertaining to your life and faith walk. As you write, expect God to respond. Be ready to be still and to listen.

CHAPTER FOUR

FEED YOUR FAITH

T his Friday's topic is to feed your faith in the midst of adversity. I have been sharing about success in my career, specifically how to connect our faith with career success in every area of our lives. My hope is that by sharing my faith journey, you too will grow in your faith in areas such as career, marriage, relationships, or any other aspect aligned with God's will. I want you to know that your faith in Christ Jesus can touch every area of your life and yield tremendous results. Our scripture reference is found in 1 Samuel 30:6-8 *(King James Bible, 1769/2017)*

"And David was greatly distressed; for the people spake of stoning him, because the soul of all the people was grieved, every man for his sons and his daughters: but David encouraged himself in the Lord his God. And David said to Abiathar the priest, Ahimelech's son, I pray thee, bring me hither the ephod. And Abiathar brought thither the ephod to David. And David enquired at the Lord, saying, Shall I pursue after this troop? shall I overtake them? And he answered him, Pursue: for thou shalt surely overtake them, and without fail recover all." (King James Bible, 1769/2017, 1 Samuel 30:6-8)

At this time, I was running an organization that was new, and needed in an area that was destitute, underserved, and under-resourced. I was a minority in this executive position—racially, sexually, and even financially—in this niche market, yet God allowed me to create this position. I was supported by individuals who wanted to see if this vision could work. I poured my whole self into it through faith, believing that God brought me there, knowing He did not bring me there to leave me.

Throughout the course of time, as I was trying to grow in this position, I had to be bold enough to believe in this promise and walk in faith. I had to know that I belonged in that position just as much as anyone else belonged in theirs. I was working with integrity; I was growing, and I was passionate about what I did. As time progressed, my testimony of promotion began to show me that this faith journey was not just flowers and roses. Faith is not about praying and snapping your fingers, as if it is a magic pill. Faith is trust. Faith is rest in Christ Jesus. Faith is growth. Faith is taking a position on the word of God that is established forever and believing it.

It is so wonderful to see how our faith in Christ Jesus can address issues of racism, sexism, or economic disparity. Our faith can handle it. As people around me in my professional field began to see the potential in my business endeavor, adversity began to rise on every side. There was more pressure and stress. God led me to a place where I was fasting every day for half a day. The more I began to fast, although I did not really know what was coming on the horizon, the more I experienced pressure and stress. I was in a unique place. I felt isolated from my former peers and colleagues in this executive position. The organization was growing, yet other individuals around me who appeared to be in positions to support me had ulterior motives and hidden agendas. Those who once supported me began to withdraw from me.

At this point, I was fasting daily, not eating or drinking, because I needed God to show up in the midst of what He allowed me to create. I needed clarity. I needed direction and instruction. The more I fasted, the more the pressure came, the more stress there was. I was driving to work one day, and God began to speak to me. The thought that came to mind was, *Feed yourself with my word.* I thought, yes, that is exactly what I am supposed to do—feed my faith! If my faith is established on the word of God, the word *is* God (John 1:1, King James Bible, 1769/2017), and the word is established forever (Psalm 119:89, King James Bible, 1769/2017) then I had to continue to feed my faith. What I feed grows, and what I starve dies. I had to allow the pressure, the stress, and the negative words around me to starve; I had to close my ears to that. I had to feed my faith.

> "FEED YOUR FAITH TO MAINTAIN YOUR SANITY, STRENGTH, AND REST SO THAT YOU WILL NOT BUCKLE UNDER PRESSURE."

Even if it was only for 15 or 20 minutes daily, I would listen to a message, a podcast, or a word from someone speaking a word of faith. The word of God was my daily bread. Literally, my daily bread!

I impress on you to feed your faith to maintain your sanity, strength, and rest so that you will not buckle under pressure, stress, betrayal, or miscommunication. Feed your faith so you can live a balanced life, maintain your peace, be edified, withstand pressure, and cultivate patience and long-suffering. Long-suffering is simply patience. You must feed your faith to avoid being worried, stressed, and/or panicked.

This faith journey is about change. It does not necessarily mean that your situation will change; it may mean that you will transform in the situation first before anything else changes.

Where God has placed you is where you belong. Whatever word of God you stood on to get to where you are now, you have to continue to feed your faith and feed that word so it may continue to establish you. When your faith grows, you receive direction and understanding in every area of your life.

God led me in that season to use faith to take risks in my career so that I could grow, be more successful, and build my character. I had to learn from some failures while experiencing some successes. I had to go through all of that to become the person I am today, so I can coach other individuals and help them develop. All aspects of my testimony and experiences are not pretty, but I have to share them so others can grow. Every time I share, I am reminded of something else that God said, and I continue to grow. This faith journey has been a multi-year journey. It does not end here; this faith journey continues.

Prayer:

Father God, in the name of Jesus Christ, for every person who reads this, I ask that you will call them, show them, and direct them to the word that you have for them to feed their faith. I pray their faith in you and your purpose for them will not die. I pray that their faith in you will direct their strategies and plans for their lives so they will grow in your word and not be discouraged. Together, we declare their purpose will not be denied, and they will walk assuredly in the area to which you have called them. I thank you, God, that you are allowing us to grow in this faith walk. I pray in Jesus' name, Amen.

Until the next Friday...

JOURNAL ENTRY

This is your opportunity to reflect, apply the scripture references to your life, list concrete ways to apply this chapter's scripture references, or ask God questions pertaining to your life and faith walk. As you write, expect God to respond. Be ready to be still and to listen.

_____

_____

_____

_____

_____

_____

_____

_____

_____

_____

_____

_____

_____

_____

_____

_____

_____

_____

_____

CHAPTER FIVE

EMOTIONS; HANDLE THEM

1 Timothy 6:11-12 (King James Bible, 1769/2017) reads, *"But thou, O man of God, flee these things; and follow after righteousness, godliness, faith, love, patience, meekness. Fight the good fight of faith, lay hold on eternal life, whereunto thou art also called, and hast professed a good profession before many witnesses."*

We are going to talk about handling emotions while holding onto our faith. It is important to address emotions in the faith journey because they can either strengthen or weaken our faith. We might mistakenly blame God, curse His promises, or deny His truth based on how our emotions lead us. Emotions can be very capricious and unstable. If we live by our emotions without grounding ourselves in the truth and faith of Christ Jesus, we will be tossed to and fro and become unstable in all our ways.

One aspect I love about the scripture *1 Timothy 6:11-12* (King James Bible, 1769/2017) is that it reminds us to be active in our faith journey. We are called to "follow after faith." Faith is not something passive or abstract. I often say it is not a miracle pill or something we access only when we want to. Faith is something we must actively pursue, engage in, and build. In previous chapters, you've read about walking in faith, standing in faith, feeding our faith, and being bold enough to believe—each of these is an active process.

The scripture in 1 Timothy says, *"fight the good fight of faith,"* which tells me there will be challenges to our faith. There will be circumstances that test it, situations that cause us to question it, and forces that try to pull us away, but it is a *good fight.* Whether we are fighting emotions or external circumstances, the fight for our faith is worth it.

When we talk about "handling" emotions, we are not referring to ignoring them or suppressing them. We are not treating emotions as enemies. Emotions are a natural and necessary part of being human, but they must be balanced and tempered by the Word of God. Achieving this balance takes effort and intentionality. Facing the depth of difficult emotions is rarely easy, but it is essential. This process, combined with fighting to hold on to your faith in God's Word, is never in vain. Your efforts have purpose—they contribute to the good fight.

> "EMOTIONS ARE A NATURAL AND NECESSARY PART OF BEING HUMAN, BUT THEY MUST BE BALANCED AND TEMPERED BY THE WORD OF GOD."

If you are:
- a believer in Christ Jesus,
- a Christian,
- walking by faith and not by sight,
- on a faith journey where your faith continues to grow in Christ Jesus,

then you know you are actively involved in the process. None of us who live by faith can passively say, "God, it's in Your hands; work the miracle." We understand that faith requires action—speaking the Word of God, aligning our thoughts with His truth, and continually evaluating our beliefs and emotions. Today, we are focusing on our emotions—how to handle, balance, and put them in perspective.

How we talk to ourselves and how we align our emotions with what we believe are integral parts of this good fight. The good fight of faith requires not allowing emotions to dictate or limit the magnitude of our faith. Emotions come in many forms: fear, frustration, discouragement, disappointment, bitterness, happiness, sadness, or joy. One day we may feel strong in our faith because we are happy, and the next day, we may feel weak because we are disappointed. Regardless of these emotional shifts, our faith must remain consistent.

This chapter is not a philosophical discourse on emotions; it is a practical exploration of emotions and faith in the context of life experiences. What happens when the things you dreamed about start to crumble? What happens when your marriage, the child you are raising, your promotion, or the dream job may take an unexpected turn? When life does not look how you envisioned and stressors emerge, you may feel isolated and begin questioning your dreams, your purpose, and even your faith in God.

You might ask:

- ◆ "Lord, am I believing You in vain?"
- ◆ "Why is this taking so much effort?"
- ◆ "Why isn't my faith producing the expected results?"

These questions arise when we think faith is something others do for us rather than something we actively participate in. Standing in faith requires effort. It involves speaking the Word of God, praying, and encouraging ourselves in the Lord to magnify His truth over the circumstances. Faith is not passive—it is an active commitment.

We must remember that while change is constant, our faith

in God's Word and His promises must not change. People, situations, and environments will change. Reflect on the Word of God and remember what people did to Jesus Christ. One day they cried, "crown Him," and the next, "crucify Him." Despite how He was treated, Jesus' faith and identity remained steadfast. As believers, we grow according to God's will and timetable. Emotions must not cause us to regress in our faith journey. Instead, we must continually check and align them with the Word of God. The fight for faith is worth it—it is a *good fight.*

In your faith journey, I encourage you to actively bring your emotions under the subjection of the Holy Ghost. In moments of stress and adversity, I've had to do the same—praying, fasting, and speaking the Word of God to remind myself of my identity in Christ Jesus. Even when circumstances didn't change as I expected, I stood firm in faith, declaring that God had made me the head and not the tail. This steadfastness is essential in the good fight of faith.

Prayer:

Father God, in the name of Jesus, give us faith, strength, and reminders to continually check our emotions. Help us to put our emotions under the subjection of the Holy Ghost and respond with the spirit of Christ, speaking Your Word above all else. In Jesus' name, we pray. Amen.

Until next Friday…

JOURNAL ENTRY

This is your opportunity to reflect, apply the scripture references to your life, list concrete ways to apply this chapter's scripture references, or ask God questions pertaining to your life and faith walk. As you write, expect God to respond. Be ready to be still and to listen.

CHAPTER SIX

TESTING OF ME FAITH

B efore we begin with our scripture reference, in each section of this journal, I have been sharing how this faith journey has been unfolding in my life, career, relationships, and other endeavors. I am still on this faith journey, and at the time of writing this book, it has been over eight years in the making.

I was a founding executive director of an organization for three interesting years before I launched any of my businesses. In the first two years, there was progress, growth, and success. However, in the last year, there were employee and fundraising challenges. The board had secretly planned to phase me out. They stopped communicating with me and supporting my endeavors. They gave me impossible goals on my evaluation, which was conducted in the middle of the year instead of at the beginning, leaving me with less than six months to turn things around. It was only by the grace of God that, in the face of opposition, we received the total funding to meet our goal two months before the end of the fiscal year. Yet, this achievement was not celebrated by my board, as they had their own plans.

In those three years, I was praised and supported during the first two, but seeds of discord were sown in the third.

Here's the irony: when I started this organization, I knew I was not supposed to remain there for more than a few years. I knew my role was to launch it to bless the participants, the surrounding community, and the stakeholders. While I was running it, my other dreams and visions were put on hold. Internally, my dreams, nonprofit and entrepreneurial ideas, books, plays, and everything creative within me began to die—and I felt it. Because of my personality, I threw myself into this venture, giving my all to grow it, and in doing so, I made what was supposed to be temporary into a permanent situation.

I began to question my faith. In the midst of new ventures, it is easy to get caught up in the present and forget what the Lord has spoken or shown you. It is not easy to change when things are going well. When things are comfortable, we like to stay there. However, when you are on a faith journey, change is a consistent part of your situation. Transformation—in you and in your circumstances—according to God's will, should be expected. Trusting and resting consistently in God is mandatory.

I forgot this truth and began to question my faith again. I asked God, "Did You call me to launch this?" I prayed, "Do not let these folks betray me or 'do me dirty.'" I questioned, "If You brought me to this, why are You changing it?" But the more appropriate question was: Was He changing it?

It was not the testing of "my" faith, but the testing of "me" faith. I had to look inward; the mirror was turned on me. I began to question, first, why I was so comfortable, and second, why I had forgotten that I was only meant to be in this position temporarily. My purpose was to launch the organization and move on to the next assignment. It was as if God spoke loudly: *Why are you trying to make something temporary permanent?*

"Check your motives," God was speaking to me during this faith journey. "Check your pride. This is not all about you. People are not betraying you—you are being propelled into your destiny."

God was saying, "I am using this experience to push you

out so you do not get comfortable." This was just like the bird that makes its nest uncomfortable so that the baby birds will leave. The discomfort and unsettling of the nest cause them to jump out and fly. The mother bird has to make the once-comfortable nest uncomfortable so the baby birds can realize their potential.

Let us review this scripture:

"Now faith is the substance of things hoped for, the evidence of things not seen." (King James Bible, 1769/2017, Hebrews 11:1)

"Now faith is the assurance of things hoped for, the conviction of things not seen." (The ESV Study Bible: English Standard Version, 2008, Hebrews 11:1)

The launching of that opportunity was the "hoped-for" thing in my life at that point. The "evidence of things not seen" was what came next. It was not

> "YOUR FAITH JOURNEY IS THE DASH BETWEEN THE 'HOPED-FOR'".

the organization I had launched; it was something more. There is a dash, a space of time, between the "hoped-for" things and the "evidence of things not seen."

Your faith journey is the dash between the "hoped-for" and the "evidence of things not seen." The faith journey is not simply completing what you set out to do. Many times, we think our faith brings us to the beginning and end of something—and that is it. In reality, it is all about the journey, the process that serves as the catalyst for our growth.

If we do not continue to grow, we stagnate. Physically, if we do not use our muscles, they stiffen and become ineffective. Similarly, our spiritual muscles, gifts, and talents will die if we do not use them. We become stagnant, like individuals in a vegetative state. As it is naturally, so it will be spiritually.

Reader, remember: Your faith journey is not where you start or where you end—it is the growth along the way. It is the dash in between. Do not make temporary situations permanent. Continue to trust and rest in God. Be willing to be transformed by the renewing of your mind in accordance with the will of God. Be okay with your situation changing, knowing that God is the same yesterday, today, and forevermore.

Prayer:

Father God, in the name of Jesus, I pray that our faith in You continues to grow; and that we will be comfortable with change because we rely on You and know that You are the only One who is the same yesterday, today, and forever. I pray that we will continue to rest and trust in You and not be shaken by changes or transformations. God, we thank You for testing us. Thank You for the testing of "us," which removes the elements that are not like You so we can be who You have called us to be. Lord, we bless Your Holy name. In Jesus Christ's name, we pray, Amen.

Until next Friday...

JOURNAL ENTRY

This is your opportunity to reflect, apply the scripture references to your life, list concrete ways to apply this chapter's scripture references, or ask God questions pertaining to your life and faith walk. As you write, expect God to respond. Be ready to be still and to listen.

_____

_____

_____

_____

_____

_____

_____

_____

_____

_____

_____

_____

_____

_____

_____

_____

_____

_____

_____

_____

_____

_____

Faith and Transformation Fridays

CHAPTER SEVEN

AMAZING FAITH

A s you work through this journal, I pray that your faith is increasing and that you are perceiving life as the Lord would have you perceive it. Are you seeing growth in your life as you process this faith journey? Are you ready to be transformed today?

Hebrews 11:3 reads:

"Through faith we understand that the worlds were framed by the word of God, so that things which are seen were not made of things which do appear." (King James Bible, 1769/2017)

"By faith we understand that the universe was created by the word of God, so that what is seen was not made out of things that are visible." (English Standard Version Bible, 2009)

Sometimes life, under God's direction, will bring you full circle to the place where you first believed in your dreams, potential, and possibilities—a time before compromise, doubt, and frustration ever took root. If you can continue on the path of faith, saying, *"God, I trust You. I cannot hear You, but I trust You. I cannot see the change, but I trust You. I am frustrated, but I trust You. It does not look like I thought it would, but I trust You"*—God will manifest Himself.

There's a powerful quote by Tony Gaskins that says: **"If you don't build your dream, someone else will hire you to help them build theirs."**

As you've progressed through this journal, you've been experiencing lessons of faith through my testimonies. I've shared my faith journey, particularly in my career and other areas of life. Regarding my career, I was on that faith journey for five years before God released me to share it with all of you. Allow me to walk you through some of the more intense parts of that journey.

In previous chapters, I shared how God blessed and professionally positioned me, elevating me to high levels. But as the storm brewing in my professional world began to intensify, faith brought about revelation. One day, I was called into a meeting with two board members of the organization I had been working with. It was a franchise birthed from an idea I contributed to, but it was not my dream or vision. I had expanded its scope in ways no one expected, and though it faced startup challenges, it progressed because of my efforts.

Before the meeting, I sought God. I remember sitting in my office and quietly asking Him, *"What should I expect?"* The Lord made it clear to me that it would be my last day with that company. Faith in God during any process brings revelation. Faith allows you to see and perceive clearly.

Hebrews 11:1 says: *"Now faith is the substance of things hoped for, the evidence of things not seen."* (King James Bible, 1769/2017)

That day, faith allowed me to see and perceive clearly. When you trust God, your faith in Him enables you to discern what has not been spoken and to be aware of things happening even when you aren't directly informed.

After that meeting, because I wasn't surprised by what was said, I left with a genuine smile and a weight lifted off my shoulders. That night, God birthed in me the vision for my own business—the full plan, name, mission, and everything! It was a for-profit entity where I would help new and emerging entrepreneurs and business leaders turn their visions into revenue and results.

I could not have conceived or birthed that plan without the separation. Staying in temporary situations can hinder your greatness from being revealed. Temporary is never meant to be permanent.

"If you don't build your dream, someone else will hire you to help them build theirs." (Tony Gaskins)

For too long, I was hired to help someone else build their dream. To pour into your plan, dream, vision, or strategy, you must first pour into your faith in Christ Jesus. This means studying His word, applying faith scriptures to your life, and immersing yourself in faith teachings. As you do this, you

"GOD'S PLAN FOR YOU WILL BE SO PROFOUND THAT IT WILL MAKE BUILDING YOUR DREAM EASIER."

will begin to see and perceive clearly, and God will map out your steps toward your calling and purpose.

God's plan for you will be so profound that it will make building your dream easier. His prescribed path will help you unlock the greatness within you that you didn't even realize was there.

Amazing faith surprises you, enabling you to conceive and birth things you never imagined you could do—and succeed at doing. Faith transforms you, allowing you to transition from one entity you thought was permanent to the next venture. Faith emboldens you and equips you to stand firm in every other area of your life.

My faith journey caused me to trust God outside my control—in my career, as I rose through the ranks, and as I led organizations. Now I can do the same for myself, other companies, and individuals. **Amazing Faith!**

"Through faith we understand that the worlds were framed by the word of God, so that things which are seen were not made of things which do appear." (King James Bible, 1769/2017)

"If you don't build your dream, someone else will hire you to help them build theirs." (Tony Gaskins)

Once you build it, they may let you go. But don't worry. If you are standing on faith, whenever separation comes, God has something greater and better for you. Amazing faith doesn't mean a life free of storms or hardships. Amazing faith leaves you in awe of God's handiwork.

When you truly stand on faith, you will be transformed—and trust me, the transformation is for the better.

Wherever you are in your faith journey, trust God. You may not always see the way, understand everything, or even like everything, but you can trust Him. Know that in trusting Him, His plan will be better than anything you could imagine for yourself.

Prayer:

Father God, in the name of Jesus Christ, I thank You for this moment with the reader. Thank You for the freedom to be transparent so that someone else can grow, be blessed, and be encouraged on their faith journey. God, You are faithful, mighty, wonderful, and holy! Cover the person reading this chapter as they process their thoughts in this journal. Surround them with Your power, love, and might. Let this word take root in their spirits and bear much fruit in their lives. It will not be plucked

up, and they will not be deceived or fall into doubt (King James Bible, 1769/2017, Matthew 13:18–23). We will stand firm on the knowledge of Your truth.
In Jesus' name, we pray, Amen.

Until next Friday...

JOURNAL ENTRY

This is your opportunity to reflect, apply the scripture references to your life, list concrete ways to apply this chapter's scripture references, or ask God questions pertaining to your life and faith walk. As you write, expect God to respond. Be ready to be still and to listen.

_____
_____
_____
_____
_____
_____
_____
_____
_____
_____
_____
_____
_____
_____
_____
_____
_____
_____
_____
_____
_____
_____

CHAPTER EIGHT

FAITH TO STAND

1 Corinthians 16:13 reads, *"Watch ye, stand fast in the faith, quit you like men, be strong."* (King James Bible, 1769/2017)

The English Standard Version reads:
"Be watchful, stand firm in the faith, act like men, be strong." (English Standard Version Bible, 2009)

A t this phase in my faith journey, God had brought me to a very unique place. I was in a position I had always dreamed of, an entrepreneurial role. I was running my own business, pursuing my endeavors, and setting my own schedule. I had clients, and projects, and made varied amounts of money depending on how much I worked—or how little I worked. I had dreamed of this professional place in life, and it was here, at this very point, where I needed faith to stand. After everything I had gone through up to that point—every stressful encounter, every learning experience and triumph, every challenge and betrayal, every victory and unexpected change—I found myself in need of faith to stand in my promise.

I needed faith to stand, to stay in position, to endure… this blessed place! Ever since I was young, I wanted to live on my own, manage businesses, and launch my creative endeavors. I had reached this place, with years of experience and success behind me, yet I needed the faith to stay there. I needed the faith to stand and endure this place.

You see, your blessed place comes with expectations. I take this moment to stress this, even at the risk of sounding redundant, to emphasize that if you are feeling this way, you are not, and will not, be alone. These feelings are valid and may be surprising, but they come at a blessed place in your life.

Whether it's your career, family, relationships, gifts, talents, or dreams, in whatever blessed area of life, your blessed place comes with expectation. The expectations could be greater maturity, or the weight of responsibility. Whatever you feel, will you trust God when your blessed place takes effort? Will you stand when you get tired? Will you read the word and encourage yourself in the Lord when

> "...YOUR BLESSED PLACE COMES WITH EXPECTATIONS."

your promise does not look like you thought? The magnitude of your blessed place can seem daunting. Sometimes the greatness in us is greater than we could ever fathom or imagine. It is at this time that we may ask, "God, can I stay here? Can I maintain this place? Can I continue to grow in this area? Can I do this?" Although your blessed place may seem daunting, YES, YOU CAN!

God's word to us in this faith journey is to have the faith to stand. This is the faith to stand on God's promises and His will for your life. The word would never have said in 1 Corinthians 16:13, *"Be watchful, stand firm in the faith, act like men, be strong,"* if we didn't need faith to attain and maintain the promises of God (King James Bible, 1769/2017). Watch, or to be watchful, is to be aware, to discern if this journey in life is in alignment with God's plan. That scripture would not have admonished us to stand fast in faith if our ability to stand would not be questioned one day. There will come a time when we may not stand firm, when our knees may start to buckle, and we may begin to question ourselves and our path. We may reach a point where we would rather sit down, take a back seat, and avoid the responsibility of walking in our calling, holding up the banner of faith, and continuing to believe in God, in ourselves, and in our gifts and talents.

This scripture is almost a "tough love" statement where the writer says, "Act like men." It says "quit like men" in the King James Version. "Be strong," but what does that mean? Do not give up; I have given you strategy, and I have given you plans. I will continue to map out ways before you—you just have to show up and be there.

I pray that you are encouraged. Know that if you are in your blessed place, it comes with maturity and responsibility. Faith in this place may be daunting, but you can handle it because you were built for it. You were created for this blessed place, and it was created for you; all you need is the faith to stand and never give up on your promise.

Prayer:

Father God, in the name of the Lord Jesus Christ, I ask that You bless all of those who read these words and that they will continue to be encouraged. I pray that they will continue to have the faith to stand, and together, we will continue to be transformed according to Your word and Your way in every area of our lives. May each of us stand firm in faith, knowing that You have greater things in store for us and that there are greater feats we can accomplish in our lives, in You, and through You.
In the name of Jesus Christ, we pray, Amen.

Until next Friday...

JOURNAL ENTRY

This is your opportunity to reflect, apply the scripture references to your life, list concrete ways to apply this chapter's scripture references, or ask God questions pertaining to your life and faith walk. As you write, expect God to respond. Be ready to be still and to listen.

_____

_____

_____

_____

_____

_____

_____

_____

_____

_____

_____

_____

_____

_____

_____

_____

_____

_____

_____

_____

_____

_____

_____

CHAPTER NINE

RENEW MY MIND,
RENEW MY FAITH

C ongratulations on making it to this point in the book. I trust you are already reaping the benefits and seeing the transformation in your life.

In the past chapters, I have referenced my faith journey through my career. Faith has demonstrated itself in other areas of my life as well. My hope is that as my faith journey continues to grow, yours will continue to grow as well. Iron sharpens iron, and together we witness the power of faith in Christ Jesus. The scripture reference today is found in Romans 12:2 (King James Bible, 1769/2017). This is the English Standard Version: *"Do not be conformed to this world, but be transformed by the renewal of your mind, that by testing you may discern what is the will of God, what is good and acceptable and perfect."*

I love that scripture because it requires us to be unique, to defy every whim, feeling, emotion, and philosophy that we encounter. It commands us to be transformed, and the way we are transformed is by the renewing of our minds.

In past chapters, I have shared physical changes that faith in action in my life has displayed. The faith journey also causes changes in the way one thinks, perceives, and envisions. In Romans, the word requires us to be transformed by the renewing of our minds and by the testing of our character. The very things that test us through the faith journey can make us question what we believe, our own abilities (as we saw in the previous chapter), and also question what the will of God is. We begin to discern the will of God. Our questions shift from our capabilities to queries such as, "God, is this your will for my life?" We build the ability to discern and ask God, "Is this good? Is this acceptable unto You? Is this Your perfect will?" The response we receive may not always be what we expect it to be. It may not be the cookie-cutter shape that we desire, but it will be the will of God (good, perfect, and acceptable).

At this time, I was operating my own business and my own non-profit. I was where I had always wanted to be. I was growing and loving the entrepreneurial experience. I was experiencing growth in the midst of this season. Then I came to the point where I began to ask the question, "Can I do this?" When I thought about where I was and where I wanted to go, or when things did not map out exactly the way I wanted them to, or when the money did not flow as consistently or as abundantly as I wanted it, this question resurfaced. You can probably attest to this. Think about when the four steps to implement your business (identification, formulation, designation, and execution) began to change, and you realized you did not like the process of those four steps. It's possible you began to realize you only want to operate in two of the four steps, or the fourth step, which is yielding the most profit, is the one you dislike the most. When it looks like you're failing in one area or changing in another, the realization may come that you have to be strengthened in an area that is most unfamiliar.

In my business endeavors, I too asked, "Can I do this?" It's easier to go back; it's easier to do something lighter and not challenge oneself, or so I thought. Can I do it? As I pondered that question and began to think about stopping, I wondered if failure is when you stop. I questioned what failure really is. Is failure when the vision does not look the way we expected? Is it that we need to be stretched or grow more? Is it the horror that we are not as great of a success as we thought we would be? Is it the realization that there is more learning to be done? Many times, the changes or unexpected events, the ebbs and flows of the process, and the growing pains tell us to reposition ourselves. We may need a new strategy to move forward.

Note, there is a transformation whenever something unexpected comes up in the place where you are prospering, in the place where you are growing, in the place where you always wanted to be. When there is an unexpected change, growth, learning process, or something fails and something else buds and grows, that is the opportunity to **"THERE IS A TRANSFORMATION WHENEVER SOMETHING UNEXPECTED COMES UP IN THE PLACE WHERE YOU ARE PROSPERING..."** be transformed. That is the testing of our faith. This is the point when we begin to discern God's will. Our thinking shifts, and we begin to think, "This is good. I did not know I needed this." You realize it may not feel great to you, but it is good for you. We get a glimpse of God's acceptable will; His perfect will for us in this process.

It is at these times you get this eureka moment when now it begins to make sense. When you personalize it and ask yourself the question, "Can I do it?", your resounding response must be, "YES, I can do it!" Yes, I can do it! It is in God's design for us. If God has shown you the vision, strategy, or plan, if He has revealed it to you and aligned your steps in accordance with it, then yes, it is according to His will for you. Yes, you can do it, but sometimes, you have to be transformed. This includes the testing of your faith, the changes, the ways that you have to be pushed and pressed a little more. The ways you are being focused are to study a little more, change your habits, or go back to the drawing board to get a new strategy, to revise the vision, to narrow down or more specifically chisel away at the mission— that is the transformation. That is the renewal of your mind that's going to transform you into exactly who God called you to be. The question you need to ask today is not "Can you do it?" The statement you should be making at this juncture is, "God, renew my mind. Renew my faith."

Remember, faith is not a magic pill; you nor I are that spoiled child that gets our "will" however we want it when we want it. Faith is that journey, that process for you to become who you are supposed to be, for that greatness to be birthed. Faith is the process of cleaning

> "FAITH IS NOT A MAGIC PILL... FAITH IS A JOURNEY."

away the extraneous stuff, the excess, the distractions, to let that shiny diamond emerge. Faith is the process of heat being turned up so that the gold can become refined and become the purest form it can. This is what happens with you. We need to stop questioning our position if we belong, and the purpose of the process, our abilities, skills, and our call. Stop, stop, stop, stop.

You are successful. You do have a measure of faith. Your faith is growing. You do have visions. You do have dreams! You are able to grow and develop in your area of business, ministry, purpose, relationship, and entrepreneurship... whatever it is, you are a success, and you can be a success! You are great. You will be great! What you need to say is, "God, renew my mind. Renew my faith." Every time you say that, every time you speak that, you build your confidence in who God called you to be. Instead of questioning yourself, make those statements, and watch God fulfill His purpose in you. Every time the imposter syndrome arises, firm up your faith with the word of God and renew your mind with the proclamations of who you are in Christ Jesus.

Faith is a process; it does not end. You never really arrive, you just continue to go from level to level, becoming who God called you to be until you fulfill every ounce of your purpose on this earth, and it is your time to take your rest. Until then, I encourage you to pray, "God, renew my mind and renew my faith." Speak and declare, "I have a renewed mind, my faith is renewed, and I am transformed in alignment with God's will."

Prayer:

Father God, in the name of Jesus Christ, thank You. Thank You for this revelation. Thank You, Lord, for reminding us that we should be praying, "God, renew my mind and renew my faith." Thank You for allowing us to recognize we are everything that You have designed us to be. We are becoming it and we are realizing it more and more as we walk out this faith journey. God, thank You for transforming us by the renewing of our minds so that we can continue to discern Your will and what is good, acceptable, and perfect unto You. Thank You for this blessing of understanding, that it will cause a transformation instantly and a new resolve in us to be everything You called us to be. In Jesus' name, Amen.

Until next Friday…

JOURNAL ENTRY

This is your opportunity to reflect, apply the scripture references to your life, list concrete ways to apply this chapter's scripture references, or ask God questions pertaining to your life and faith walk. As you write, expect God to respond. Be ready to be still and to listen.

_____

_____

_____

_____

_____

_____

_____

_____

_____

_____

_____

_____

_____

_____

_____

_____

_____

_____

_____

_____

_____

CHAPTER TEN

FAITH—THE SIXTH SENSE

I was studying the five senses and I was amazed because the senses send signals to the brain, and the brain tells the senses what it is experiencing. The eyes take snapshots of images and send those images to the brain, and the brain says, "Oh, you see a boy, you see a sun, you see a fence." Our ears send sound to our brain, and our brain says, "You heard them say, 'Hi, how are you?'" Everything from our touch, our smell, to our taste buds sends the sensations, scents, or flavors to the brain, and our brain says, "That feels hot, smells pungent, or tastes sweet." What was amazing to me as I studied is that we use one of our senses, if not all, every day. They work even while we are sleeping. They work together to let our brains know what is occurring around us. The senses keep the brain alert, and therefore, we are safe and protected by the warnings or information they send about our environments.

Okay, I am a little excited and amazed because, as I was studying about the senses, God gave me a revelation about faith and, more specifically, faith in Him. With faith in God, we can have the spirit of faith (King James Bible, 1769/2017, 2 Cor. 4:13), we can have the fruit of faith (King James Bible, 1769/2017, Gal. 5:22), the gift of faith (King James Bible, 1769/2017, 1 Cor. 12:9), and it has the ability to grow so much greater in God (King James Bible, 1769/2017, Mark 4:31-32). If you are a believer in our Father God, the Lord Jesus Christ, and if you believe in the word of God, then you have the ability to operate in that level of amazing faith and to see faith manifested. We are called to faith; it is our sixth sense. Christians, yes, the Bible says we're in the world but not of it (King James Bible, 1769/2017, John 15:19). Here is a little alien moment: you do not have five senses, you have six! The same way our five senses are supposed to operate in the natural, our faith—the sixth sense—is supposed to operate in the spiritual, to manifest in the natural.

That is an awesome glimpse of the operation and movement of our senses. Our senses never tell our brains what they are experiencing. Our eyes do not tell the brain, "We are seeing a boy and a girl." It just says, "Brain, here are pictures." Our taste buds do not say, "I am tasting something salty." They just send the flavor to the brain, which says that it is salty or sour. If we can take a hint from the five senses and say, "God, I see this

"WE ARE CALLED TO FAITH; IT IS OUR SIXTH SENSE."

in my life, please tell me what it is," so many times we take labels and say, "God, the doctor says it is cancer; God, someone says it is death; someone said I can never be in that position; others say my plan will never amount to anything." Whatever it may be, we take labels to God, and that is why our life is out of order and the promises and expectations of our faith are not manifested. This is the reason we are seeing things differently from how God has predestined them. We place a label on what we experience and then tell God, "I need you to fix that [label]." That is the action we are taking, instead of saying, "God, this is what I'm seeing. What is it?" If we functioned in our faith according to the proper operation of senses, we would wait for God to actually tell us, "It's no big deal. It's not as it appears. Just relax and trust Me. This trial is going to strengthen you."

God may say, "This is what you are going through, and this is what you are going to experience. This is the evil the enemy means it for, but this is what I am going to let the outcome be." He will tell us what we are seeing and experiencing. When we see as He says, our lives align with His will.

Faith is our sixth sense. We are to take any word, any thought, any experience, and take it to God. God is our "brain"; He is our "controlling center." He is supposed to be operating through us every day, which means there is no room for doubt, self-proclamations, or speculation. Our sixth sense, faith, is supposed to work while we are sleeping. In moments when we are not watching, may be unaware, taken by surprise, or not expecting something, our sixth sense should be at work. When we have built our faith so much through prayer, studying the word of God, listening to God, and speaking the words of promises and faith, when we have put muscle on our faith, even in moments when we may not be on alert, our faith is supposed to work. Our sixth sense should consistently work in every area of our spirit, soul, mind, knowledge, influence, and emotion to let us know what is occurring around us. Faith protects us when we are unaware. Faith sends signals and information to our brains and spirits, redirecting our attention to the direction of the Holy Ghost within us. The Holy Ghost will warn, prepare, and guide us about what is in operation around us.

> "FAITH SENDS SIGNALS AND INFORMATION TO OUR BRAINS AND SPIRIT, REDIRECTING OUR ATTENTION TO THE HOLY GHOST WITHIN US."

Reader, from previous chapters, there were times when faith showed me, warned me, and revealed things to me. Faith allowed me to hear what my ear was not hearing in the natural.

That was the faith sense operating. When you lose one of your senses, your body compensates. "...if one cortical area is deprived of its normal sensory inputs during early stages, it will be reorganized by the nondeprived senses in a process of cross-modal plasticity that not only increases performance in the remaining senses when one is deprived but also rewires the brain, allowing the deprived cortex to process inputs from other senses and cortices..." (Bengoetxea, et al., 2012; Patel et al., 2018). When someone is blind, their sense of touch can be extremely sensitive, and they can hear better than they can see. If you lose your hearing, your taste may become stronger, and your sight may be stronger. Your senses compensate for the others.

As it is in the natural, so should it be in the spiritual. We are to operate in faith at all times. If we are operating in doubt or unbelief and we are

> "WHEN FAITH IS NOT OPERATING, ANXIETY IS RAMPANT."

not operating in faith, then our other five natural senses will compensate and become heightened. When your natural man operates without faith, all your natural man is going to give you is a natural response, a carnal response. When faith is not operating, anxiety is rampant. What we see will rule us rather than what we believe the Word of God says. As children of God, we have six senses. If we do not operate in our sixth sense, faith—the spiritual one—the other natural senses will always get stronger and dominate. If this happens, we will never see the manifestation of God's will. Consequently, we will never get stronger in God, and our relationship may diminish or be severed as a result. I am encouraging you to operate in your own sense. Great people of God, Christians in the body of Christ, you have six senses, and faith is your sixth sense.

Ephesians 2:8 says, *"For by grace you have been saved through faith. And this is not your own doing; it is the gift of God"* (King James Bible, 1769/2017). Our five senses are an automatic part of our physical design, a package deal. We are born with a measure of faith (trust). The gift, spirit, and fruit of faith—the sixth sense—comes with being a child of God. The moment we believe in Jesus Christ and become born again, we have the ability to operate in the fullest capacity of faith. Firstly, as Christians, we have *a measure of faith* (King James Bible, 1769/2017, Rom. 12:3). If we believe in Christ Jesus, we are able to grow in faith; our faith is in God, and it is not of ourselves. Great and awesome people of God, if you are wondering why we are not as strong as we are supposed to be, why we have not experienced things that we are supposed to experience, it may be because our natural senses have dominated, and we have not been operating in our sixth sense.

Faith, as an operable sixth sense, comes to warn, protect, reveal, manifest, and give access to greater spiritual experiences in this life with Christ Jesus. It is a sense we are born with, have access to, and grow the more it is nourished with the Word of God. Operating in our sixth sense, faith heightens our spiritual acumen, dulls our natural sense, and aligns us with the supernatural power of God.

Prayer:

Father God, in the name of Jesus Christ, I ask that You cover every reader, every person who handles this book, and every word that has been spoken, that it will not be corrupted, interrupted, or disturbed in any way. Let Your word take root on good ground in our spirit, that it manifests and may bring forth the power of faith in our lives. Let us operate in faith in every moment. Let that sixth sense be sharpened, so that our five senses will never have to compensate for the lack of faith. I ask this and I ask that You cover everyone under Your blood to continue to be strengthened in the power of Your might. We declare that nothing, no one, no situation, no contract, no plan, no block can be devised against us and against this word for our lives. I pray this now in Jesus' name, Amen.

Until next Friday...

JOURNAL ENTRY

This is your opportunity to reflect, apply the scripture references to your life, list concrete ways to apply this chapter's scripture references, or ask God questions pertaining to your life and faith walk. As you write, expect God to respond. Be ready to be still and to listen.

_____

_____

_____

_____

_____

_____

_____

_____

_____

_____

_____

_____

_____

_____

_____

_____

_____

_____

_____

_____

CHAPTER ELEVEN

UNDERSTANDING THE JOURNEY

Faith, according to the Merriam-Webster dictionary, is defined as complete trust or confidence in someone or something; a strong belief in God; or a strongly held belief without question. Hebrews 11 defines faith as *"the substance of things hoped for, and the evidence of things not seen"* (King James Bible, 1769/2017). If you walk by faith, and every human being has a measure of faith, you do not operate by your senses alone—what you see, hear, or feel (Rom. 12:3, King James Bible, 1769/2017). Faith itself is the evidence of the very thing that you hoped for, not the actual thing you desire.

What happens when you struggle with the subject of faith? Let us think about school: when you struggle in a subject, you do not have the option to give up and still be successful. Some may give up and fail the class, needing to repeat it, or they may decide they are ready to commit and learn the subject in order to succeed in executing the information. When you know there is no space to give up, what do you do when you struggle? You get extra help, study more, practice, and apply the information frequently for effective recall. The reality is you will always struggle with something. The irony is that when we struggle in our faith, and it gets difficult or the wait is extended, we may give up, turn back, or feel that our faith efforts are all for naught. Others may choose not to believe God's word and instead walk in a faithless way, choosing to have faith in human ability rather than in God. In the natural world, when we struggle with any subject, we do not settle for the limited knowledge that we have; we study more to attain full understanding of the content.

During the course of your faith journey, when you do not understand everything, do not give up. Study faith scriptures more, recite, quote, and pray faith scriptures and the promises of God. Begin saying to God, "Your word says this…" Give Him back His word in prayer. He is faithful to perform His word. When you read the scriptures, ponder to whom God is speaking. Think about the context. Does that promise or word apply to everyone? If it does, tell God, "This applies to me; this is your promise. I do not see where it was just for one set of people, and I have yet to see it manifest in my life." As you begin to study the word and give it back to God, you free God to move in your life, if you believe in Him to do so.

It's important to understand this faith journey in order to successfully and effectively stay the course. Hebrews 11 tells us:

- By faith, we obtain a good report;
- Through faith, we understand;
- By faith, we offer unto God;
- By faith, one can be translated from one state of being to the next;
- Without faith, it is impossible to please God;
- By faith, you can be warned of God, moved, prepared, or made into an heir of God;
- By faith, we can receive a preconceived plan for direction.

God can reveal things to us. He can map out ways and plans for us.

- By faith, you can stay in your place of promise;
- You can be brought to your wealthy place;

- You can be brought to your place of purpose and destiny;
- Through faith, you can receive strength to produce;
- If you stop believing and hoping, you won't produce;
- By faith, you can bless others;
- By faith, you can prophesy;
- By faith, you can be protected;
- By faith, you can take a stand;
- By faith, you can let go of things;
- By faith, you can experience a miracle;
- Through faith, you can subdue kingdoms, obtain promises, and stop devastations.

This is Hebrews 11. When you're on your faith journey, trying to understand the journey, wondering what you are able to access and perform through faith and by faith, I encourage you to begin reading this chapter. It is here we gain a fuller understanding of the power of faith.

"THE EFFICACY OF YOUR FAITH AND HOPE DEPENDS ON WHOM YOU PLACE IT."

Do not allow people to tell you not to believe in God or that there's nothing to faith. We will have faith in other things. The same people who tell you not to believe in God will tell you to believe in yourself, in them, or in what you can see or feel. They are going to tell you to believe in something. Without faith in something, life is hopeless. The efficacy of your faith and hope depends on whom you place it. According to Romans 12:3, we are created to have a measure of faith (King James Bible, 1769/2017). I sat down in a chair and did not check to see if the screws were tight. I had faith that it would hold me up because that is what it is created to do, and secondly, because it held me before. In the same way, I encourage you to trust and exercise your faith in the Lord Jesus Christ as you are on your faith journey. Faith is created to work for you and bring God's word to reality for you. If you have ever tried God, faith has worked for you before. I do not know what it is—maybe it's your finances, maybe it's trying to get through school, trying to find a spouse, salvage your marriage, create a business, release your patent, or maybe it's trying to bring forth a child. Whatever you are hoping for and trusting for, stand firm in your faith in what God's word has promised you.

To say that you are a person of faith is to say that you have complete trust, a strong belief, and confidence in God. As you experience life and its unexpected turns, stand on your strongly held belief in God's word without question. That is the time to ask God to show you how to operate in your faith, how to align your desires with His, what to pray for, and that what you pray does not take you outside of God's will.

It is about understanding your journey. Many times, we hinder ourselves from growth—from becoming who we are supposed to be—because of unbelief. Doubt causes us to give up, stop believing in God, struggle in our hope in the Word of God, and question who God said we would be. Doubt becomes unbelief and is the enemy of hope and faith. Any tool we use, any new experience, any content or information we hope to obtain calls for understanding. If we are to operate fully in whatever we handle, we have to learn and understand it. This is the same for faith; we need to study faith to understand how to use it effectively.

For this Faith and Transformation Friday, I am encouraging

you to challenge your mind to study to understand faith and to walk in faith, so that you can be sustained in Christ Jesus in this journey called life. You will continue to live until you stop taking your last breath. You can live your fullest life, or you can live a life that is incomplete, mediocre, or beneath your purpose.

I encourage you and challenge you to be changed according to the word of God today. I encourage you to study the scriptures to understand faith so you can walk in the fullness of faith in God. You can be strong in your faith journey, regardless of whatever situation or devastation arises. Remember, through faith, you can subdue the very thing that seems greater than you and obtain the promises that belong to you. Through faith, you can stop the greatest devastations. This is a call to study, to strengthen your knowledge of faith in God, to be firm in this journey, and to hold onto your strong belief in God's word without question. Understanding the faith journey is about the people of God sharpening each other to withstand the opposition of the enemy. The enemy is after your faith.

"THROUGH FAITH YOU CAN STOP THE GREATEST DEVASTATIONS."

Today, declare with me: "We want our minds to be changed and our wills to be encouraged to study the word of God and seek the face of God. We will trust, believe, and study to understand the faith journey to continue walking in our calling, purpose, and potential. We will remain consistent in this faith journey in life, and we will not stop believing God's promises for our lives or the purpose for which we were created."

Prayer:

Father God, in the name of Jesus Christ, I pray that you allow our understanding to grow and open up the eye of our enlightenment according to your word. May we understand that we will grow in the very word that you illuminate in our minds and hearts. We can be who you called us to be! We declare we will not give up, we will not stop believing in God. We will not stop having hope because we will strive to understand faith, to walk fully in faith, to live by and through it. In this journey, in Jesus' name, we pray, Amen.

I hope this was another encouraging Transformation Friday! Continue to trust God and know that you are a person with purpose and potential, and it can be fulfilled. You can do all things through Christ who strengthens you (Phil. 4:13, King James Bible, 1769/2017)!

Until the next Friday…

JOURNAL ENTRY

This is your opportunity to reflect, apply the scripture references to your life, list concrete ways to apply this chapter's scripture references, or ask God questions pertaining to your life and faith walk. As you write, expect God to respond. Be ready to be still and to listen.

_____

_____

_____

_____

_____

_____

_____

_____

_____

_____

_____

_____

_____

_____

_____

_____

_____

_____

_____

_____

CHAPTER TWELVE

APPLY YOUR FAITH

As I traveled my faith journey through my professional experiences, I began to see that what I learned about faith in one area of my life had to be transferred into other areas. We are to apply what we learn through faith to all aspects of our lives. The faith lesson we learn in one situation can be applied to another. Will you remember to take those life lessons into the next situation? I had to think about what I had learned. I realized that through all the tests, trials, triumphs, promotions, challenges, separations, growth, and wonderful opportunities in my professional career, I had learned to fast and pray. I learned to feed myself with the word of God and specifically the word of faith daily. I learned to stand on God's promises, to believe in who He called me to be, and to allow my faith to be renewed by the word of God. I learned to be bold enough to believe and to walk in the faith of God.

These were the life lessons from that time period in my professional life when my faith had to be applied. The same year that I separated from my executive position, I launched my own business and celebrated my first wedding anniversary. It had been a full and wonderful year, but my husband and I had not conceived a child. At the time, we wanted a little baby of our own. That year, we experienced our first pregnancy and our first miscarriage. The next year, we were excited to experience our next pregnancy. Our child was growing in my womb, but our sweet child died in my 35th week of pregnancy. I had experienced loss before, but never to that magnitude. I had experienced loss through career changes, relationships, and friendships, but never the loss of life in this way.

I had to think, "What in faith did I exercise? What had I learned before that I exercised in my most devastating moment?" When my son's life was essentially gone, and the doctors had to induce my labor, I asked God, "Can you still bring him back?" I had to think and use the words of faith, and I had to pray. In reality, I was so overcome by my situation that although I recited the scriptures of faith and prayed, in hindsight, I needed in that moment a community of believers. When you go through any situation, even when you are applying what you've learned from one situation to the next, you need a community of believers around you. When you cannot pray or speak for yourself, you

> "WHEN YOU GO THROUGH ANY SITUATION...YOU NEED A COMMUNITY OF BELIEVERS AROUND YOU."

must have someone in your ear saying, "God can do all things"; "We are going to believe Him to the end"; "We are going to pray according to God's abilities"; "He is able to deliver." However He decides to deliver, you need a community of believers who will still say, "We will still bless God"; "We are going to praise Him"; "We are going to make our request known"; "We are going to touch and agree about what we are believing until God says otherwise."

Who do you believe? You must pray until something happens, until the thing you want happens. You must know that whatever the result is, it is governed by what God says. Will you pray until that comes? These are some of the things I learned because the reality is that when you are operating in faith, you will face different levels of challenges, some greater than the last. You have to be determined that you have no other option except to believe God and to believe God for what you are praying to see.

Now, I didn't see what I was praying for. I was praying for God to return life to my son so that I could birth him into the world, that he would be a miracle of life. I did not see that. I have been forever changed as a result. I have not become an unbeliever. No, not changed to doubt! I learned that I had to build up my faith even more. I learned that each test was trying my faith on another level. I had to realize that although my son did not live, I might have learned through this experience how to build my faith, to be the faith community for someone else. If their child is threatened with death or they are in a point of devastation, I will pray and believe with them until we see what we pray for, or until God says it is finished.

"Jesus answered and said unto them, Verily I say unto you, If ye have faith, and doubt not, ye shall not only do this which is done to the fig tree, but also if ye shall say unto this mountain, Be thou removed, and be thou cast into the sea; it shall be done. And all things, whatsoever ye shall ask in prayer, believing, ye shall receive." (King James Bible, 1769/2017, Matthew 21:21-22)

This was the scripture I struggled with as I grieved and returned home without my son in my arms. I was wounded and hurt. I could not understand why this had happened to me at this point in my life. During these times, I would come across this scripture, and I would struggle with it because I did not receive what I asked or prayed for. Yet, this is the very scripture I am giving to you. This is the very scripture I stand on because I am a believer that we pray according to God's ability. We do not let our experiences dampen our faith. What happened to me may be the very thing I needed for my faith to become strong, so that I can pray for someone else through their struggles. I would never say the loss of a child is something you need, but I'm talking about what it has become. This may be the very learning experience that enables me to stand in agreement with somebody else and pray with them that they will see what they are praying for. As long as their prayers align with God's will, we will agree to stand firm, and we will not allow doubt or anything else to come into the midst of our prayer request. The very scripture I struggled with before is the scripture that I fight so much more to see, Matthew 21:21-22, not only in my life but in the lives of other people.

Ask God what His will is, pray your request, and ask that your prayer request aligns with God's will for you. Recognize that God's will is sovereign and trust His ability in your situation. There is no room for doubt! There is no need for YOU to doubt. I prayed for my position, and the doors opened. I prayed for the business to be launched, and it was. I prayed, "God, do not let these people betray me or try to steal what I created or what I'm trying to do." The betrayal happened, but God warned me beforehand; He was my sixth sense. He allowed me to see because my faith was aligned with Him. He allowed the steps to be made, and because He allowed me to see in advance, He enabled me to go and negotiate for my settlement. I stood firm in Him, and because I did, He opened doors for my businesses. There were things I expected, and things I did not, but all things worked out for my good. It all had an expected end. I want you to understand that there is no uncertainty in God. It is not a guessing game with Him. There is no coincidence in God. You will have an expected end. Things may not always map out the way you expect them to because we may want what is comfortable or easy. The things that will work out will work out for your good.

The three Hebrew boys in the scriptures always stand out to me. They said, "God is able to deliver us, King Nebuchadnezzar, out of your hands, and He will deliver us out of your hands. He is able to deliver us from the fiery furnace, and He will deliver us from your hands." I interpret that as an affirmation that God is able, and He will! They spoke about His ability and the fact that He will do it. I imagine their attitude being one of, "Come what may," (I'm paraphrasing), we are not going to bow down to you. However God decides to deliver, we are going to trust Him and believe Him. Whatever He decides to do for us in the moment is best. For the Hebrew boys, it became a miracle that they were delivered from the fiery furnace and from the hand of Nebuchadnezzar, alive without any harm or danger. They did not even smell like what they went through. It was a miracle, yes, a miracle. And sometimes we look for just those miracles. Are we ready to be the ones to say, "Come what may, we will trust?" That's what this is about. Applying your faith means saying, "Come what may, I will trust God." I trust God for my job, my husband, my child, and my family member's healing. Whatever it is, you trust, and you apply your faith to every area of your life.

I've shared different aspects of the faith journey in my life, and no, it has not been just professional. The journey has been in that area, but it has also been in multiple other areas. I continue to grow, I continue to trust God, and I continue to believe God that my experiences align with His will.

Today, I encourage you to continue to apply your faith across every area of your life. Stand firm on Matthew 21:21-22; do not let your circumstances alter your faith. Let your faith align with God's ability and His will, what He will do and what He's able to do. Stand firm and believe!

Prayer:

I pray right now in the name of Jesus that your faith is strengthened according to the word of God and not your own experiences. That you are able to apply your faith and what you have learned in other areas of your life. Move forward in faith and not backward in doubt, unbelief, worry, lack of concern or lack of understanding. In Jesus' name, Amen.

Until next Friday...

JOURNAL ENTRY

This is your opportunity to reflect, apply the scripture references to your life, list concrete ways to apply this chapter's scripture references, or ask God questions pertaining to your life and faith walk. As you write, expect God to respond. Be ready to be still and to listen.

_____

_____

_____

_____

_____

_____

_____

_____

_____

_____

_____

_____

_____

_____

_____

_____

_____

_____

_____

_____

CHAPTER THIRTEEN

ANOINTED ASSASSINS

Before we dive into this chapter, I feel the need to give this disclaimer. First and foremost, I am not a terrorist, not a threat to my government, nor am I a threat to the kingdom or the body of Christ. I am, as you are, a threat to the kingdom of darkness, and this is what we are called to be. This is the power we have as children of God and Christians; we are anointed assassins.

Daniel 2:16-17,49 is a very interesting chapter. It reads: *"Then Daniel went in, and desired of the king that he would give him time, and that he would shew the king the interpretation. Then Daniel went to his house and made the thing known to Hananiah, Mishael, and Azariah, his companions. Then Daniel requested of the king, and he set Shadrach, Meshach, and Abednego over the affairs of the province of Babylon; but Daniel sat in the gate of the king."* (King James Bible, 1769/2017)

I chose this scripture because, if you are familiar with the text, the king at the time had a dream, and he could not remember the dream, but it troubled him. He called for all the soothsayers, astrologers, and anyone else you can think of, to tell him the dream and its meaning. They said they could not, and he responded by saying, *"Well, kill all the wise men."* Daniel sought time. This was interesting to me because Daniel did not pray to God first and say, "Can I go to the king and ask for time so that you will show me what the king's dream is?" Not at all. He quickly went to the king and said, "Give me time, and I'll show you your dream and the interpretation." He was that confident in the God of his salvation and the God he served. He knew that, because this was such a serious situation and God is able to do everything, all he had to do was ask, and God would do it. This is a formula we should all follow.

Daniel then went to his house and made the matter known to his other brothers in God, his Israelite brothers of the tribe of Judah—believers who also said, "We will not defile our bodies with the king's meat." Those like-minded brothers, who believed firmly in God, were the ones Daniel went to and made the issue known. They stood together, touched and agreed, and prayed. Daniel made his request, and God made the dream known to him.

Look at this faith formula in action:

1. Daniel spoke according to God's ability, in faith and confidence.
2. He went to his community of faith to inform them of what was happening and touched and agreed with them.

As a result, God showed him the king's dream and gave him the interpretation. King Nebuchadnezzar said, *"Daniel, surely your God is the God of all gods and is the true God."* This demonstration of power through faith by God resulted in God being glorified, and Daniel was promoted. You have to understand the magnitude of this promotion. The children of Israel were taken into captivity. They were an enslaved people, under the control of Babylon as a result of Israel's backsliding from God. In the midst of captivity, those who took a stand for God were promoted and blessed. King Nebuchadnezzar put Daniel over the affairs of his estate. Daniel said, "Do not take me alone" (paraphrase). Who do you think Daniel brought with him? He took his community of faith: Shadrach, Meshach, and Abednego (also known as Hananiah, Mishael, and Azariah). They were set over the affairs of the province of Babylon; they were all promoted.

This tells me when:

♦ You stand in faith, even if it is not something for yourself but something for someone else,

♦ When God shows up and works according to His ability,

♦ You touch and agree, and pray in the earth according to the will of God,

it is done in the earth. You also will be blessed as a result of your exercise of faith. The formula of faith is:

♦ Make the declaration,

♦ Touch and agree with fellow believers, and

♦ Wait with expectation.

Daniel made a declaration about God's ability; he touched and agreed with his community of faith and waited with expectation. He did not expect God to fail. As a result, God answered and revealed the secret things, the things that are not easily seen. God revealed them based on Daniel's faith.

People of God, if you are a person who is trying to grow in your faith in God, if you are already a Christian, and if you are already solid in your faith and want to continue to grow, there is something you need to realize: the believing Christian, the believer, is a faith activator, and you are unique. In a previous chapter, I shared with you that we have six senses, and your sixth sense is faith. Well, I heard a pastor say something that resonated with my spirit: the Christian does not just have four seasons, but the Christian has five seasons, and the fifth season is the due season. You must recognize that, because you have a sixth sense you must operate in at all times, which is faith, and because you have a fifth season, the due season, you can stand and know that there is a season that comes to you. Whatever you ask, according to God's promises and His will, believing it in Jesus' name, will be released to you. It's due unto you because you are operating in faith. This should strengthen your faith, just as the other four seasons—winter, spring, summer, and fall—come, your due season MUST come, and you will not miss a year without your due season!

> "WE HAVE BEEN ANOINTED TO ANNIHILATE DOUBT AND UNBELIEF IN EVER AREA OF OUR LIVES."

Let me tell you why we are called anointed assassins. We have been anointed to annihilate doubt and unbelief in every area of our lives. Wherever doubt is, faith cannot manifest. It is impossible to please God without faith. If the enemy can influence you enough to doubt (that is all he has to do), then you block your own power in the word and the power and ability of God. You block it by simply doubting or having a moment of unbelief. That is why it is important for you not only to wash yourself with the word of God and decree the word of faith daily but also to have a community of faith standing with you. Just when you become a little bit overwhelmed by your situation, your community of faith should begin to speak into your ear the word of faith, the promises of who God is, and what God said belongs to you. That word of faith resonates in your heart and strengthens your faith. You have been anointed to assassinate doubt and unbelief in every area of your life and in any way that it reveals itself. It is God's will to heal; it is God's will to make you whole; it is God's will to manifest His promises in your life, corporately and individually. He will not operate in unbelief. Understand that you can operate, talk, and declare according to God's ability; you can pray according to His will. You can touch and agree with your community of faith and wait with expectation, knowing that God will answer. Every way doubt and unbelief try to rear their ugly heads, you have the power to rebuke them by the blood of Jesus, in the name of Jesus, with the word of God, and by the word of faith. You can assassinate unbelief and doubt because you have been anointed to do so.

I pray that this was an encouraging chapter about faith and transformation. As you grow in your faith journey, you begin to change and become transformed. I continue to seek God to strengthen me in the word of faith so I can stand on His word, as you stand on His word, and together we grow in this faith journey.

Prayer

Father God, in the name of Jesus Christ, I ask that you cover this chapter and that those who read it are changed by it under Your blood, Your power, and Your anointing. We pray against any interference, interjections, or hindrances to the manifestation of the power of Your might and the Word through this chapter. I pray that this chapter blesses the lives of many people. I speak and declare that godly faith communities arise and abound according to Your word, and the anointed assassins rise up even as these words are prayed. God, be glorified, let Your power be manifested, and You be magnified in every way. In Jesus' name, we pray, Amen.

Until next Friday...

JOURNAL ENTRY

This is your opportunity to reflect, apply the scripture references to your life, list concrete ways to apply this chapter's scripture references, or ask God questions pertaining to your life and faith walk. As you write, expect God to respond. Be ready to be still and to listen.

_____

_____

_____

_____

_____

_____

_____

_____

_____

_____

_____

_____

_____

_____

_____

_____

_____

_____

_____

_____

_____

CHAPTER FOURTEEN

POWER OF FAITH - PART. 1

I believe in God's word because I have seen God's word in my life. I have seen the manifestation of His word just recently, and it has changed my life. Since the passing of my son, which is one of the experiences I have shared, I have been on a quest to tap into the power of faith, to see my faith in the word of God and my faith in the promises of God manifested. The Lord led me to this scripture, and it reads:

"And saying, Lord, my servant lieth at home sick of the palsy, grievously tormented. And Jesus saith unto him, I will come and heal him. The centurion answered and said, Lord, I am not worthy that thou shouldest come under my roof: but speak the word only, and my servant shall be healed. When Jesus heard it, he marveled and said to them that followed, Verily I say unto you, I have not found so great faith, no, not in Israel. And Jesus said unto the centurion, Go thy way; and as thou hast believed, so be it done unto thee. And his servant was healed in the selfsame hour." (Matthew 8:6-8, 10, 13, King James Bible, 1769/2017)

This text is interesting because there is a blueprint here, and as the children of God, we can implement this blueprint. Once we do, we will begin to operate in the complete power of faith in God, and we will see it manifested immediately. In this scripture, the centurion went to the source for help—he went to Jesus Christ. Jesus made a promise, He said, "I will come," which means God will come and meet our needs. Wherever God comes, wherever God shows up, He doesn't show up as an observer; He comes to do and to manifest. The centurion recognized the authority of Jesus Christ. He reverenced Him, and he had faith in His ability. His faith was so strong that he said to Jesus, "You don't even have to come to my house; as a matter of fact, I am not worthy that you would come; JUST SPEAK!" God was so impressed with that level of faith and reverence. The word of God says that Jesus marveled. That's how impressed God was with this man's faith. He said, "As you have believed, according to your faith." How he believed—that's how the healing was manifested. The healing did not happen when the centurion was on his way or when he returned home; the moment that he said to Jesus, "Speak the word, and it is done," it was done!

If we could just follow this blueprint, we would begin to transform according to the will of God. Our faith would explode and would be manifested in the earth. True miracles, signs, and wonders will be worked. People will say, "Truly, the God we serve, the Lord and Savior Jesus Christ, is real and true because of the signs, miracles, and wonders that follow." Let me give you the blueprint. The scripture said Jesus said unto him, "I will come and heal him."

1. That's the promise.

Secondly, the centurion said, "But speak the word only, and my servant will be healed."

2. That's the activation of faith.

God's response to that type of faith: "He marveled." He had not found such great faith in all of Israel.

3. God responds according to our faith.

There is an automatic response to our faith: it invokes the presence of God to respond, to look, and to be drawn into our situation. The same measure of faith that we operate in, that allows us to declare and seek the face of God to speak according to His ability, is the same measure in which we have to continue to operate. How we believe is how the manifestation is performed in our lives. The result in the text is that the centurion's servant was healed, his prayers were answered, and the miracle was manifested.

How do we know the operation and declaration of faith is according to God's will? The text stated, "I will come and heal him." God will do what He said He would do and is capable of doing. This is the blueprint.

Prayer:

Father God, in the name of Jesus Christ, thank you. Thank you for this calling to increase our faith; thank you for your word enriching us; thank you for reminding us who we are in you. Thank you that we can trust you, and faith in you is real and sure. Thank you for reminding us that your word is established forever. Thank you for the power of faith and for manifesting the power of faith in our lives. God, I ask that you cover these readers with your love, with your power, and with your blood, Lord Jesus Christ. I pray that there will be no interferences, hindrances, blockages, or retaliating spirits/assignments against their growth in you, Lord Jesus Christ. Together we declare, we will grow and operate in faith. We will see the power of faith manifested in our lives. In Jesus' name we pray, Amen.

Until next Friday…

JOURNAL ENTRY

This is your opportunity to reflect, apply the scripture references to your life, list concrete ways to apply this chapter's scripture references, or ask God questions pertaining to your life and faith walk. As you write, expect God to respond. Be ready to be still and to listen.

_____

_____

_____

_____

_____

_____

_____

_____

_____

_____

_____

_____

_____

_____

_____

_____

_____

_____

_____

_____

_____

CHAPTER FIFTEEN

POWER OF FAITH - PART II

I f you have made it to this chapter, you have traveled with me on this faith journey. My prayer and hope are that in my transparency, you too will be strengthened in your own faith journey.

I used to wonder why my faith did not "work" at times. Why did it not work to resurrect my son in my womb and make him whole? Why did it not work, specifically, when the doctors proclaimed him to be dead and I said, "No, he will live and not die"? Why did my faith not work? That is where I truly was, for quite some time. I wondered if I doubted or if I had given up. I questioned whether I should have had all the prayer warriors surrounding me in prayer, on the phone, virtually, or in person. This conversation played out in my head for a long time. It propelled me to seek the efficacy of faith in my life because I do believe! I believe in Christ Jesus! I believe in the word of God! I believe in the word of faith.

> "And the apostles said to the Lord, 'Increase our faith.'
> So the Lord said, 'If you have faith as a mustard seed, you can say to this mulberry tree, 'Be pulled up by the roots and be planted in the sea,' and it would obey you." (Luke 17:5-6, NKJV, 1982)
> "Then the disciples came to Jesus privately and said, 'Why could we not cast it out?' So Jesus said to them, 'Because of your unbelief; for assuredly, I say to you, if you have faith as a mustard seed, you will say to this mountain, 'Move from here to there,' and it will move;

and nothing will be impossible for you. However, this kind does not go out except by prayer and fasting.'" (Matthew 17:19-21, NKJV, 1982)

Mustard seed faith... if you have ever seen a mustard seed, you know it is tiny. Yet, the Lord references mustard seed faith more than once. The reference to "mustard seed" faith is not about the quantity of faith but about the potency of faith in Christ Jesus in our lives. It demonstrates the extreme power of faith. When we exercise faith that has the ability to grow greater than itself, miraculous things can happen. If we operate fully in the complete measure of faith that we have, we will see our faith manifested. Complete faith in the ability of Christ Jesus in our lives is extremely powerful!

You know, I pondered this notion a lot. I said to myself, "What do I have to do to see my faith grow as a mustard seed? How can I operate in this area of faith more? How can I activate this area of faith more? What do I need to do to see what I am requesting or proclaiming be done and fulfilled?" In asking these questions, it has been the concept of the seed that God has been ministering to me.

In Luke, when the apostles said, "Increase our faith," Jesus talked about the potency of faith with the mustard seed example. In Matthew, when the disciples asked, Jesus identified their unbelief and then spoke about the potency of faith, the mustard seed, and the necessity of prayer and fasting to strengthen our faith and witness the manifestation of God's ability in our lives. There is a formula; a way that people who have been successful and have operated in the full power of faith have seen their requests manifested. There are steps that are extremely important:

- They spoke and believed according to God's ability.

- They did not allow the magnitude of the situation to bring doubt and unbelief into their lives.
- They declared God's will in their lives.
- They declared, "God will do it for us"!

The three Hebrew boys, as recounted in Daniel 3:16-18, stated their victory would happen because God is able to do so. Their connection and loyalty to God were so strong that, whether He did it or not, they knew God was going to deliver them out of Nebuchadnezzar's hands, however, it would be done. God says throughout His word to:

- Operate in the full power of faith;
- Just believe, do not doubt;
- Pray and fast to strengthen your faith so that unbelief cannot arise.

You must stand on the amount of faith you have completely until God says otherwise. If He does not say, "It is finished," "Not so," or "Not My will," then you stand on the word of God and the word of faith and believe for what you have requested. God will keep you and sustain you. He will let you know if it is His will, if it is not His will, if it is His plan for your life, or if it is not His plan for your life.

We are children of God through Christ Jesus; Christ Jesus is the seed of Abraham, and we are the seed of Christ Jesus (Galatians 3:14-18, King James Bible, 1769/2017). Everything that was promised to Abraham belongs to us as children of the Most High God. We can stand on the promises of God and believe because God is faithful and just to keep His promises.

Prayer:

Father God, in the name of Jesus Christ, I pray that people are blessed by this chapter and share it with others who will be encouraged. Those who may be discouraged, disappointed, or overwhelmed by their situations will be encouraged by faith in Your word, right now, in the name of Jesus. God, You are able to do miraculously, and You will manifest Your promises in our lives. We give You all the praise and glory now. In the name of Jesus, we pray, Amen.

Until next Friday...

JOURNAL ENTRY

This is your opportunity to reflect, apply the scripture references to your life, list concrete ways to apply this chapter's scripture references, or ask God questions pertaining to your life and faith walk. As you write, expect God to respond. Be ready to be still and to listen.

CHAPTER SIXTEEN

THERE IS HOPE

R eader, these last few Fridays, whether weekly or monthly, have been a journey—a walk that has been unraveling emotions, thoughts, and questions, as well as the Word and promises. Like you, I continue to grow. God is good; God is worthy. I must say that God has been doing great things in my life. He has opened up doors, provided new opportunities, and financial blessings, released healing, and manifested peace and contentment (contentment alone is deliverance). I encourage you to be encouraged by those things. There are still some things that I am waiting for and looking for God to do. It is a wonderful thing to know that God is the one who works the impossible. There are some impossible things in our lives, but He is the one who works the impossible. There is hope!

"For there is hope for a tree, if it be cut down, that it will sprout again, and that its shoots will not cease. Though its root grow old in the earth, and its stump die in the soil, yet at the scent of water it will bud and put out branches like a young plant" (The ESV Study Bible: English Standard Version, 2008, Job 14:7-9).

This tree is grown, it is an adult, but it is able to put out branches like a young plant. This represents a new birth, a new budding tree—newness! God can bring your life full circle. "If it's been put down," situations may have worn you down, you may be depressed, discouraged, or not seeing change. You may even be forgetting the blessings of God and the past deliverances of God. The daily walk of life, or your process, may be wearing you down. 'If it is cut down, it will sprout again.' This is a promise to you concerning your faith, your dream, your purpose, and your plans that line up with the will of God. The good thing is that God will not withhold from you—it will sprout again. That is His promise. The Word says that 'if the root grows old'... If you feel like life is passing you by or you are too old, remember there is no age to your purpose. Don't believe that lie. Regardless of how long you have been waiting, the Bible says, at 'the scent of water,' that means the opportunity may not be present yet, the money does not have to flow yet, the blessing does not have to materialize yet, the healing may not have manifested yet—all you need is the possibility of what God will do. All you need is a possibility to hold on to

"DO NOT ALLOW ANYTHING TO CUT DOWN YOUR BELIEFS, YOUR FAITH, OR YOUR TRUST IN GOD."

(that is faith), and you will bring forth. You will see the healing of God, you will see the manifestation of your dreams. All you need is hope.

There is hope. Do not allow anything to cut down your beliefs, your faith, or your trust in God. Don't let the time or the wait wear you down. Don't let 'that your roots are old' make you believe that what you were established in, what your foundation was founded on, is old and outdated. Do not believe that. The Bible says that you will sprout again—you will! There is a revival coming to you, there is hope.

A pastor made a comment, and when he preached this, it resonated with my spirit. In the midst of Job's tragedy, God did not allow the enemy to attack his mouth so he could not speak or attack his mind so he could not think (G. Carswell, personal communication, February 2018). Regardless of how difficult your situation is, if you are not in some insane asylum somewhere or in a straight jacket restrained where you cannot think or function, then there is hope. God has still given you the capability of your mind to think, to process the word of God, and to search the Scriptures—that is your hope. If your mouth has not been shut, you can still speak, and you can praise God. You can still set the atmosphere that God can dwell in, is attracted to, and can work in. Where God is, miracles can happen. Where God is, unclean things cannot dwell. If you still have the fruit of your lips—your praise and your worship to God, in the name of Jesus—and you have the full use of your mind, faith has not been destroyed. Your tragedy cannot take your faith. You are able to speak life into your faith. You are able to remember that there is hope. All you need is that possibility, and as your faith grows and manifests, so will the promises of God.

> 'ALL YOU NEED IS THAT POSSIBILITY...AS YOUR FAITH GROWS AND MANIFESTS, SO WILL THE PROMISES OF GOD."

No matter how long we have been waiting, or if we see blessings in one area of our lives and not another, God is faithful, and God is still just! There is hope. As I write this chapter, this is my situation right now. I am not telling you something from last year. In the midst of God blessing me, I have to remind myself, saying, "God, you just blessed me here, so God, if you blessed me here, then you will bless me in other areas." I will not stop believing! I will continue to stand firm and believe in the word of the Lord.

Prayer:

Father God, in the name of Jesus, thank you for the possibility. Your word says, "Ask and it shall be given" to us. We stand knowing there is still hope. Encourage the very person reading this that there is hope, so their faith may grow. God, You are well and alive; You are good, and Your mercy endures forever. Thank you, Jesus! Amen.

Until next Friday...

JOURNAL ENTRY

This is your opportunity to reflect, apply the scripture references to your life, list concrete ways to apply this chapter's scripture references, or ask God questions pertaining to your life and faith walk. As you write, expect God to respond. Be ready to be still and to listen.

_____

_____

_____

_____

_____

_____

_____

_____

_____

_____

_____

_____

_____

_____

_____

_____

_____

_____

_____

_____

REFERENCES

Bengoetxea, H., Ortuzar, N., Bulnes, S., Rico-Barrio, I., La-fuente, J. V., & Argandona, E. G. (2012). Enriched and deprived sensory experience induces structural changes and rewires connectivity during the postnatal development of the brain. *Neural Plasticity*, 2012.

English Standard Version Bible. (2008). *ESV Online.* https://esv.literalword.com/

King James Bible. (2017). *King James Bible Online.* https://www.kingjamesbibleonline.org/ (Original work published 1769)

Patel, T. S., Mehta, A. S., Patel, N., & Mali, N. (2018). Comparative study of simple auditory reaction time between congenitally total blind people and normally sighted controls. *National Journal of Physiology, Pharmacy and Pharmacology, 8*(12), 1697-1697.

www.ingramcontent.com/pod-product-compliance
Lightning Source LLC
Chambersburg PA
CBHW071526120626
46550CB00006B/2369